May 2016

# A Rebalanced Transatlantic Policy toward the Asia-Pacific Region

PROJECT DIRECTORS
Heather A. Conley
Ernest Z. Bower

AUTHORS
Heather A. Conley
James Mina
Phuong Nguyen

A REPORT OF THE CSIS EUROPE PROGRAM AND CHAIR FOR SOUTHEAST ASIA STUDIES

CSIS | CENTER FOR STRATEGIC &
INTERNATIONAL STUDIES

ROWMAN & LITTLEFIELD

Lanham • Boulder • New York • London

## About CSIS

For over 50 years, the Center for Strategic and International Studies (CSIS) has worked to develop solutions to the world's greatest policy challenges. Today, CSIS scholars are providing strategic insights and bipartisan policy solutions to help decisionmakers chart a course toward a better world.

CSIS is a nonprofit organization headquartered in Washington, D.C. The Center's 220 full-time staff and large network of affiliated scholars conduct research and analysis and develop policy initiatives that look into the future and anticipate change.

Founded at the height of the Cold War by David M. Abshire and Admiral Arleigh Burke, CSIS was dedicated to finding ways to sustain American prominence and prosperity as a force for good in the world. Since 1962, CSIS has become one of the world's preeminent international institutions focused on defense and security; regional stability; and transnational challenges ranging from energy and climate to global health and economic integration.

Thomas J. Pritzker was named chairman of the CSIS Board of Trustees in November 2015. Former U.S. deputy secretary of defense John J. Hamre has served as the Center's president and chief executive officer since 2000.

CSIS does not take specific policy positions; accordingly, all views expressed herein should be understood to be solely those of the author(s).

## Disclaimer

This publication has been produced with the assistance of the European Union. Its contents, however, are the sole responsibility of the authors and can in no way be taken to reflect the views of the European Union.

© 2016 by the Center for Strategic and International Studies. All rights reserved.

ISBN: 978-1-4422-5947-8 (pb); 978-1-4422-5948-5 (eBook)

Center for Strategic & International Studies
1616 Rhode Island Avenue, NW
Washington, DC 20036
202-887-0200 | www.csis.org

Rowman & Littlefield
4501 Forbes Boulevard
Lanham, MD 20706
301-459-3366 | www.rowman.com

# Contents

# Acknowledgments

The authors and project directors would like to thank a number of individuals for their considerable contributions of time, expertise, insights, and intellect to this project over the past two years. Specifically, we thank current and former U.S. officials and experts: Ambassador Jon Huntsman, Admiral Samuel Locklear, Deputy Secretary Richard Armitage, Dr. Amy Searight, Michael Fuchs, Laura Stone, Andrew Quinn, Angela Ellard, Matthew Palmer, and Charlie Cook. We are also grateful for the contributions of our European partners: Ambassador David O'Sullivan, Gunnar Wiegand, Moreno Bertoldi, Peter Potman, and Klaus Botzet. We also thank Ambassador Pham Quang Vinh for his participation in our project. We were fortunate to draw upon the knowledge of our CSIS colleagues who were enthusiastic participants in this two-year project: Scott Miller, Mike Green, Sarah Ladislaw, Matt Goodman, and Chris Johnson. We also would like to thank our colleagues from the EU Delegation to the United States, both past and present, for their outstanding collaboration: Francois Rivasseau, Caroline Vicini, Konstantina Kostova, James Barbour, Tim Rivera, and Michal Safianik. Finally, we also thank current and former members of the CSIS Southeast Asia team—Benjamin Contreras, Kathleen Rustici, Elke Larson, and Murray Hiebert—for their contributions, as well as Europe Program interns Eric Adamson and Pierce Tattersall for their assistance in preparing the final report. It goes without saying that all the participants' insights shaped and guided our final report. Finally, we thank the Delegation of the European Union to the United States for their generous financial support of this project.

# Executive Summary

In November 2011, Secretary of State Hillary Clinton publicly outlined the Obama administration's pivot to Asia. Due to criticism over the term "pivot," the administration declared that its policy was an effort to "rebalance" its strategy toward Asia. Although the United States had certainly focused on the Asia-Pacific region in the past, this public policy assertion represented a shift in American foreign policy by boldly proclaiming that the twenty-first century would be "America's Pacific Century." The rebalancing strategy sought to increase American investment in the Asia-Pacific region through diplomatic, economic, and strategic channels while supporting the development of a more durable regional security and economic architecture to promote stability and prosperity in the region.

But not all parties welcomed America's Pacific rebalancing policy. Sensing that the United States was prioritizing Asia over the needs and interests of other regions, America's European allies, whose partnership has been a pillar of U.S. foreign policy since the end of the Second World War, perceived the shift as a pivot away from its Atlantic orientation, which contributed to anxiety within European capitals. In hindsight, both Europe and the United States were in the process of rebalancing their policies toward Asia, which created new and important opportunities for the United States and European Union to jointly address Asia's economic, political, and security evolution within an international legal and normative framework.

Both the United States and European Union share similar interests and objectives in the Asia Pacific. Trade and investment are key components for both U.S. and EU policy, and both have launched ambitious negotiations with regional partners to liberalize trade with East Asia's burgeoning economies and reinforce international trade standards. Both the European Union and United States have invested in the development of the 10-country Association of Southeast Asian Nations (ASEAN) bloc to strengthen international norms, legal practices, and institutional capacity. But fully exploring the region's vast economic potential requires a stable and predictable regional security environment at a time when international norms are being challenged.

In light of these clearly aligned interests, there was a concerted effort to engage senior EU policymakers in a sustained dialogue during the first Obama administration. Former Assistant Secretary of State for East Asian and Pacific Affairs Kurt Campbell made it one of his priorities to engage more strategically with Europe about U.S. Asian policy. European ambassadors in Washington were regularly briefed on U.S. policy and encouraged to get Europe involved in the region. One significant outcome of this engagement was the development of deeper institutional ties between the European Union and ASEAN as well as an EU-ASEAN ministerial dialogue in 2012. Another area of significant transatlantic policy success was coordination vis-à-vis Myanmar. Following the removal of U.S. and EU sanctions on Myanmar, the Obama administration pledged $75.4 million in aid for FY 2014. Within the auspices of the first Myanmar-EU Forum in June 2013, the European Union announced that the organization's largest aid program for an Asian country would be set up for Myanmar in the next few years.

Yet despite this precedent for consultation and the positive results it produced, since 2012 the United States and European Union appear to have pursued independent and at times competitive policies in the Asia Pacific. Neither Washington nor Brussels has yet identified a systematic way or a formal consultative mechanism to align their respective Asia-Pacific strategies, and have worked together in the region only when it is expedient or when clear policy divergences occur. Consequently, U.S. and EU policies have on occasion hindered rather than enabled the other's policy objectives and impeded the realization of mutual strategic interests. As both the European Union and the United States deepen and widen their economic and security engagement with the Asia-Pacific region, how can the transatlantic relationship be used more effectively to accelerate the region's economic development while ensuring the highest international economic standards, strengthening the region's institutional architecture, and following international legal principles?

In 2014, the Europe and Southeast Asia Programs at the Center for Strategic and International Studies (CSIS) embarked upon a two-year initiative to create a new and enduring EU-U.S. collaborative mechanism to enhance transatlantic Asia Pacific policy coordination and understanding. Through a series of quarterly briefings that brought senior U.S. government officials, congressional staff, and area experts together with European ambassadors and senior diplomats, CSIS aimed to enhance transatlantic understanding about the Asia-Pacific region, enhance mutual policy awareness, and facilitate essential contacts between EU and U.S. officials.

Substantively, the topics addressed focused on economic developments in the Asia-Pacific region, including trade and energy; the domestic and regional consequences of China's evolution; and the evolving security dynamics in Southeast Asia, particularly surrounding international maritime disputes. CSIS also hosted two public conferences featuring senior U.S. and European officials to analyze these regional dynamics and identify areas where Washington and Brussels can more effectively work together to magnify their mutual policy impact. In particular, these sessions dedicated considerable policy attention to assessing how the transatlantic relationship can work more effectively in the economic and security space while strengthening ASEAN's role in the region. This report is the culmination of this two-year study and presents the findings of our research while also offering actionable recommendations for U.S. and EU policymakers.

## Summary of Key Findings

### U.S.-EU Economic Engagement in the Asia-Pacific Region

- Washington and Brussels have powerful and common strategic interests in ensuring that the highest international trade and investment standards and liberal economic values are maintained in this dynamic region. Thus far, the United States and European Union have preferred to maintain divergent trade policy approaches toward Asia or to cooperate with each other on an ad hoc basis when convenient. This approach has come at the expense of a unified, principled, and norms-based strategic vision for the region and its future.

- The United States and European Union have pursued different trade strategies in Asia. While the United States has preferred to utilize a regional, 12-country Trans-Pacific Partnership (TPP) framework to enhance its trade and investment rules-based and regulatory framework, the European Union has opted to "bilateralize" its trade relationship with individual Asia-Pacific countries.

- U.S. policy has sought to strengthen Asian regional institutional architecture based on international legal norms and values to maintain U.S. influence in the region to the exclusion of China. The European Union takes a different approach, seeking to deepen its economic engagement with China while expanding its bilateral and institutional engagement with the region. However, both the United States and European Union are pursuing bilateral investment treaties with China.

- The lack of a transatlantic consensus on trade and investment standards may impact Europe's ability to advance its own trade agenda as the TPP becomes institutionalized over time in the Asia Pacific. As Asian partners increasingly point to TPP as a template for free-trade talks, European leaders may not be prepared to accept U.S. trade and investment standards in sensitive trade areas.

- Transatlantic policy divergences vis-à-vis China have also impacted efforts to respond to Beijing's increasing assertiveness in the region. The United States wants to see China emerge as a responsible and engaged global partner and to see its policy framework based on a comprehensive assessment of China's role in the region. The European Union and its largest member states see themselves first and foremost as economic actors in Asia, as Brussels compartmentalizes its economic relationship with China to protect it from negative political repercussions related to Beijing's human rights violations or regional behavior. Because Brussels "does not pursue a geopolitical agenda" in the region, it typically does not express its views on difficult political issues.

## Transatlantic Perspectives on Asia-Pacific Security Cooperation

- The United States and the European Union share a common foreign and security policy vision for the Asia-Pacific region: to uphold peace and stability, ensure respect for international law and principles as well as institutions, and safeguard the unimpeded flow of commerce in maritime Asia.

- Across the region, international norms and rules are increasingly being challenged, which has a destabilizing effect on the region. Both the United States and European Union have a strategic imperative to ensure that international norms and values are managed and upheld in the security sphere, and it is in their mutual interest to work together to maintain and reinforce Asia's emerging security architecture.

- For decades, the United States has maintained robust permanent military and naval deployments in the region and has sought the engagement of its European allies to help strengthen the international legal and institutional regime in Southeast Asia.

Despite their shared vision for the region, the European Union and the United States have not always acted in concert to jointly defend these common interests.

- While the European Union has stated that it aims to establish itself as a credible security actor in the Asia Pacific, it has done little to achieve this objective. The European Union possesses limited oversea power-projection capabilities, and in practice European interest in maritime security developments in the region has not gone beyond diplomatic statements.

- The European Union does not view itself as a geopolitical actor in Asia, yet it is a direct beneficiary of the U.S. naval presence and open sea lines in the South China Sea at a time when EU countries are expanding economic and diplomatic engagement in the region. Given relatively anemic European defense spending and its limited ability to project conventional military forces in Asia, it is unrealistic to believe that European countries will play a significant security role in Asia but Europe can and should play a larger role in reinforcing international legal norms and potentially imposing costs should international law be violated.

- When the 28 countries of the European Union speak out on an international issue, the message carries significant international reputational weight and can be particularly powerful in reinforcing the importance of international legal norms and codes of conduct when they are violated. This policy voice is amplified when used in concert with the United States.

- Individual EU member states (notably the United Kingdom and France) maintain a higher degree of strategic interest in the Asia Pacific as a consequence of their colonial legacies and overseas territories and play a minimal but important security role in the region. This engagement can help to promote a stronger EU role in the region.

## Policy Recommendations

### Recommendations for Strengthening EU-U.S. Economic Cooperation in Asia

- *Create a Structured Dialogue Regarding China's Market Economy Status (MES)*. Greater policy prioritization and urgency must be given to the creation of a U.S. and EU structured dialogue to consult over granting MES to China.

- *Develop a Joint Vision for Trade Policies in Emerging Sectors*. The U.S. and EU trade negotiators should identify and then develop a roadmap for areas where international trade rules are scarce in the Asia-Pacific region.

- *Prioritize Dialogue on Asian Economics at the G7 Summit*. As a leading international forum that discusses geo-economic and geostrategic issues and brings together the United States, European Union, and Japan, the G7 is a natural arena to deepen and enhance EU-U.S. economic cooperation in the region.

- *Establish a Transatlantic Dialogue on ASEAN Connectivity*. Consideration should be given to developing a dedicated consultative mechanism related to EU and U.S. initiatives on enhancing ASEAN's connectivity and infrastructure to avoid duplication and to ensure that the highest international trade, investment, and transparency standards are met.

- *Trilateralize Transatlantic Consultations with ASEAN*. Consideration should also be given to developing a trilateral U.S.-EU-ASEAN consultation on an annual basis.

## Identifying New Opportunities to Strengthen EU-U.S. Cooperation in Asia-Pacific Security

- *Prepare a Joint Statement on the Outcome of the Tribunal of the Permanent Arbitration Court in The Hague*. The forthcoming ruling of the Arbitral Tribunal in The Hague in response to the Philippines's claim against China could be an important and fast-approaching opportunity to issue a joint EU and U.S. statement in support of international maritime law.

- *Initiate a Renewed EU-U.S. Diplomatic Push for the Completion of a Maritime Code of Conduct*. Following the Arbitral Tribunal ruling, the United States and European Union, with ASEAN members, should revitalize the pursuit of a maritime code of conduct.

- *Increase the Number of European Countries Participating in the 2016 RIMPAC Exercises*. Expanding European participation in Pacific exercises will help to enhance naval cooperation between European countries and their Asian partners and send a strong signal that the European Union is interested in seeing that freedom of navigation is upheld in the region.

- *Initiate an EU-U.S. Costs Imposition Consultation in Response to Violations of International Law*. Should violations of international maritime law continue and if maritime disputes are settled by force in the South China Sea, there should be a discussion of joint efforts to impose costs on the parties that violate international law.

- *Consider Trilateralizing EU-U.S.-ASEAN Cooperation on an International Rules-Based Approach*. EU interlocutors should be invited as observers to U.S.-ASEAN meetings with participation in supporting the development of regional institutional architecture and strengthening legal norms.

- *Create a Permanent Asia-Pacific Consultation at the G7 Leaders Level*. The members of the Group of Seven should create a permanent agenda item related to political, economic, and security developments in the Asia-Pacific region to develop shared understanding and joint solutions.

- *Expand European Participation in Southeast Asian Antipiracy Efforts*. EU participation in existing efforts would provide an opportunity for Brussels to share its valuable expertise and enhance its contribution to Asian maritime security.

- *Consider European Membership of the Expanded ASEAN Maritime Forum.* In 2012, ASEAN launched the Expanded ASEAN Maritime Forum. While the United States currently participates in this dialogue, there is presently no European participation.

01

# Strengthening EU-U.S. Economic Engagement in the Asia-Pacific Region

## Introduction

The Asia-Pacific region is one of the most economically dynamic regions of the twenty-first century.[1] Over the past decade the region has boasted unmatched economic growth, expanding by an impressive 6.5 percent in 2015 and 6.8 percent in 2014. This rapid development has translated into immense benefits domestically (private wealth in the Asia Pacific multiplied by 29 percent in 2014) and has helped the region improve its participation in global markets.[2] At a time when the developed, postindustrial economies in the West are struggling to generate new economic growth, the region has become a major driver of global growth. Nearly two-fifths of all new economic activity is now generated in East Asia,[3] and by 2050 the Association of Southeast Asian Nations (ASEAN) bloc of countries is expected to be the world's fourth-largest economic group.[4] This robust performance and extraordinary potential, combined with its large population and untapped markets (the 10 ASEAN countries alone are home to 620 million people), makes Southeast Asia an attractive source of trade and investment opportunity. For these reasons, the United States and the European Union have actively sought to deepen their economic ties with the region over the past several years.

Since President Barack Obama articulated the United States' foreign policy rebalancing toward the Asia Pacific in 2011, the U.S. government has prioritized the Asia-Pacific region on its foreign policy agenda, particularly focusing on enhancing regional economic architecture and initiatives and participating in regional forums at the highest levels of government. Most notably, in 2015 the United States concluded a historic free trade agreement with 11 other Pacific Rim economies, the Trans-Pacific Partnership (TPP). The United States has also prioritized Asian dialogue at the most senior levels, as evidenced by President Obama's consistent participation at regional forums. President Obama attended the Asia-Pacific Economic Cooperation (APEC) forum in Manila in November 2015 and he hosted ASEAN

---

[1] The European External Action Service defines the Asia Pacific as including the entirety of the Asian continent beginning in Pakistan, India, and Afghanistan, whereas the U.S. Department of State refers to East Asia and the Western Pacific region.
[2] "The wealth of nations: Asia-Pacific is wealthier than Europe," Free Exchange Economics Blog, *The Economist*, June 17, 2015, http://www.economist.com/blogs/freeexchange/2015/06/asia-pacific-wealthier-europe.
[3] World Bank, "East Asia Pacific Economic Update, October 2015: Staying the Course," October 2015, http://www.worldbank.org/en/region/eap/publication/east-asia-pacific-economic-update.
[4] Vinayak HV, Fraser Thompson, and Oliver Tonby, "Understanding ASEAN: Seven things you need to know," McKinsey & Company, May 2014, http://www.mckinsey.com/industries/public-sector/our-insights/understanding-asean-seven-things-you-need-to-know.

leaders in Sunnylands, California, in February 2016, which reaffirmed the U.S.-ASEAN strategic partnership (announced at the November 2015 Kuala Lumpur summit) as well as Washington's commitment to maintain regular head of state/government contacts with ASEAN leaders at the annual East Asia Summit (EAS).[5] But U.S. policy toward Asia has not solely been about trade, dialogue, and strengthening regional forums. Substantial democratic progress has been made in Myanmar following a historic election on November 8, 2015. This program was supported by strong U.S. and European engagement and enforcement of a sanctions regime. Myanmar's transition, though incomplete, has reduced an impediment to regional institutional development.

As the United States has sought to rebalance its policy toward Asia, senior EU officials have noted that the European Union has similarly refocused its policy efforts on the region, but that it also "never left." Since 1996, the European Union has participated in the Asia-Europe Meeting (ASEM) biennial dialogues. During the most recent summit in 2014, themed "Responsible Partnership for Growth and Security," members exchanged views on economic, financial, regional, and global issues, as well as traditional and nontraditional security challenges.[6] The European Union is the largest donor to the ASEAN Secretariat, and has worked closely with ASEAN as its economic and institutional integration progresses through the €15 million ASEAN Regional Integration Support from the EU (ARISE) program between 2012 and 2015.[7] On January 1, 2016, the ASEAN Economic Community (AEC) took effect, creating a single Southeast Asian market that closely resembles the European single market. The European Union is quick to note, however, that it is not forcing its institutional model upon the region, but rather sharing best practices. Accordingly, the AEC is not expected to lead to a monetary union or deeper political integration.

But there are transatlantic differences in policy approach, particularly in trade. While the United States has preferred to utilize a regional framework (TPP) to enhance its trade and investment rules-based and regulatory framework, the European Union has preferred to "bilateralize" its trade relationship with the Asia Pacific. In 2011, the EU-South Korea FTA entered into force, and negotiations with Singapore and Vietnam concluded in 2015. Brussels is also negotiating with Japan, the Philippines, Thailand, and Malaysia over preferential trade agreements.[8]

Both the European Union and United States, however, have focused on enhancing infrastructure connectivity in an effort to drive regional development and integration. In the 2015 EU-ASEAN joint statement, the European Union reiterated its commitment to deepening Asian connectivity, not only through infrastructure development but also by helping to remove other barriers such as regulatory red tape and the vast income and

---

[5] Office of the Press Secretary, "Joint Statement of the US-ASEAN Leaders' Summit: Sunnylands Declaration," news release, White House, February 16, 2016, https://www.whitehouse.gov/the-press-office/2016/02/16/joint-statement-us-asean-special-leaders-summit-sunnylands-declaration.
[6] "Responsible Partnership for Sustainable Growth and Security: Final Chair Statement," Proceedings of 10th Asia-Europe Meeting Summit, Milan, Italy, October 17, 2014, http://www.aseminfoboard.org/sites/default/files/documents/2014_-_ASEM10_-_Chair_Statement.pdf.
[7] European External Action Service, "The EU-ASEAN Relationship in Facts and Figures," May 19, 2015, http://eeas.europa.eu/factsheets/news/eu-asean-relationship_factsheet_en.htm.
[8] European Commission, "Overview of FTA and Other Trade Negotiations," February 2016, http://trade.ec.europa.eu/doclib/docs/2006/december/tradoc_118238.pdf.

development gap between Southeast Asian countries to facilitate closer policy coordination.[9] Toward this end the European Union has pledged to triple its aid to the Lower Mekong countries between 2014 and 2020 to €1.7 billion. Similarly, the United States has recently announced a "U.S.-ASEAN Connect" initiative that will focus on strengthening economic ties between U.S. and regional businesses as well as improving the investment climate. This initiative will see the creation of regional hubs to coordinate and advance U.S. engagement in four areas—business, energy, innovation, and policy.

Despite this level of activity and commitment to work closely with ASEAN countries to deepen trade and economic cooperation, there are inherent limits to this cooperation due to weak trade and investment standards and protections that are incompatible with Western requirements, as well as many countries' limited experience with democratic governance, rule-of-law, and free-market standards. Moreover, there exists a wide range of economic, labor, and environmental development standards among ASEAN countries. For example, only 4 out of the 10 ASEAN countries are members of TPP. Yet despite these obstacles, greater region-to-region economic contacts between ASEAN and the United States and Europe, as well as more intensive trilateral engagement to enhance ASEAN's liberal, rules-based underpinnings, can accelerate the region's economic and institutional development that are foundational elements toward "building a new Asia."[10]

## The Geopolitics of Asian Economics

While some view the extensive U.S. and European outreach to ASEAN and greater free-trade arrangements such as TPP and the European Union's FTAs as a way to spur rules-based and normative regional economic growth, others see these policies as a counterweight to China's increasing use of its growing regional economic strength to influence its neighbors. Just as the United States and Europe have deepened their trade engagement with the region, so too has China. Beijing signed a free-trade agreement with ASEAN in 2005 and has experienced a significant increase in regional trade. As much as 12 percent of all Malaysian exports go to China, and between 6 and 8 percent each for Singapore, Thailand, and Vietnam, respectively.[11] After more than a decade of growth above 7 percent (China's GDP slowed to 6.8 percent in 2015 according to official statistics), Beijing enjoys considerable influence over regional economies and commerce. ASEAN countries also enjoy being part of China's global supply chain, which provides new opportunities and benefits.[12]

As China seeks to translate its growing regional economic weight into political and diplomatic influence, its economic policies have increasingly come into conflict with liberal

---

[9] European Commission, "Joint Communication to the European Parliament and the Council: The EU and ASEAN: A Partnership with a Strategic Purpose," May 18, 2015, http://eur-lex.europa.eu/legal-content/EN/TXT/PDF/?uri=JOIN:2015:22:FIN&from=EN.

[10] Gunnar Wiegand (keynote remarks at "Strengthening EU-U.S. Cooperation in the Asia-Pacific Region" conference, CSIS, Washington, DC, February 17, 2016), http://csis.org/multimedia/audio-strengthening-eu-us-cooperation-asia-pacific-region.

[11] Organization for Economic Cooperation and Development (OECD), *Economic Outlook for Southeast Asia, China and India 2016: Enhancing Regional Ties* (Paris: OECD, 2016), 28, http://dx.doi.org/10.1787/saeo-2016-en.

[12] Matthias Bauer, Fredrik Erixon, Martina Ferracane, and Hosuk Lee-Makiyama, "Trans-Pacific Partnership: A challenge to Europe," Policy Brief No. 9, European Center for International Political Economy (ECIPE), November 2014, http://ecipe.org/app/uploads/2014/12/PB09_1.pdf.

market norms and values—putting Beijing at odds with the United States and Europe. China has been reluctant to comply with the standards set by the World Trade Organization (WTO). Although China has committed to implementing a series of reforms to align with WTO standards following its accession to the organization 15 years ago, the Chinese economy continues to be heavily influenced by a high degree of government intervention and centralization. Chinese state-owned firms and industries have enjoyed preferential benefits thanks to repeated and generous state and local subsidies, investments, and alleged currency manipulations (which have also skewed economic data, altered trade flows, and created industrial over capacity, which depresses markets).

Consequently, China has been internationally criticized for its economic policy and trade behavior, and developed economies (such as the United States) have understandably hesitated to reform existing international economic governance institutions (like the International Monetary Fund) to allow China to have greater voice. In response, Beijing increasingly seeks to create alternative institutions and new instruments in order to exert greater regional influence, redefine the rules of economic engagement in Asia, and shape the future economic policy landscape to China's benefit (which has had the added benefit of challenging the American-dominated global economic order). Several European countries expressed early support for these alternative instruments. A perfect example of this is China's decision to launch a $100 billion Asian Infrastructure and Investment Bank (AIIB) in 2015 to rival the U.S.- and Japanese-dominated Asian Development Bank (ADB) and World Bank as the premier development agencies in the region. In part due to a lack of transatlantic policy unity regarding the rules-based framework and transparency surrounding the AIIB, the United Kingdom, Germany, and other EU members signed onto the AIIB while the United States declined to participate.

In 2013, Beijing has also launched a Eurasian investment campaign known as the "One Belt, One Road" (OBOR) initiative. Envisioned as "a modern Silk Road," OBOR will increase the connectivity of China to the rest of Eurasia (extending as far as Moscow and Rotterdam) through infrastructure investments in roads, railways, ports, oil and natural gas pipelines, and other infrastructure projects. Since its initial introduction, OBOR's scope has expanded to include the "promotion of enhanced policy coordination across Asia, financial integration, trade liberalization, and people-to-people connectivity."[13] Similarly, China is actively seeking to conclude free-trade agreements across Asia, such as the Regional Comprehensive Economic Partnership (RCEP). RCEP is in some ways a response to the U.S.-led TPP regional trade framework. It is clear that Beijing is attempting to redefine the terms of engagement among the region's largest economies—including key trade partners Japan, South Korea, ASEAN, and India—in Beijing's favor.

Not only do these developments directly challenge transatlantic unity and leadership in global economic governance, international financial institutions, and regional trade agreements, but they are rapidly eroding and weakening American and European international legal norms, principles, standards, and national economic interests. If China successfully refashions the rules of economic engagement and liberal trade and investment

---

[13] Scott Kennedy and David A. Parker, "Building China's 'One Belt, One Road,'" *CSIS Critical Questions*, April 3, 2015, http://csis.org/publication/building-chinas-one-belt-one-road.

standards for itself and the Asia-Pacific region, the West may be forced into a position of readjusting its own high international labor and environmental standards to preserve its share of global trade and investment in the future—as well as its global influence.

Given these high stakes, Washington and Brussels have a powerful and common strategic interest in ensuring that robust standards and liberal economic values are maintained in this dynamic region. Unfortunately, to date the United States and European Union have pursued independent trade policies in the Asia-Pacific region.

U.S. policy has sought to strengthen Asian regional institutional architecture based on international legal norms and values to maintain U.S. influence in the region but this has occurred largely to the exclusion of China despite Washington's steadfast insistence that U.S. policy does not seek to contain or exclude Beijing. The European Union, on the other hand, simultaneously (and at times preferentially) has sought to deepen its economic engagement with China while increasing its bilateral and institutional engagement with the region. The European Union and its largest member states see themselves first and foremost as economic actors as Brussels "does not pursue a geopolitical agenda" in Asia.[14] What is left unsaid is that it is the responsibility of the United States to play (and pay for) a larger security and geopolitical role vis-à-vis China to ensure regional stability and open sea-lanes (particularly in the South and East China Seas), from which the European Union benefits but neither participates nor incurs political or economic costs.

Rather than resolving these policy differences and seeking to develop a broader transatlantic strategy toward Asia, the United States and European Union have preferred to cooperate with each other on an ad hoc basis when convenient—such as on implementing economic sanctions and working to improve democratic standards in Myanmar—but not when individual economic or security stakes are high, such as over the AIIB or the contentious maritime disputes in the South China Sea. As Washington and Brussels advance their separate interests, it has come at the expense of a unified, principled, and norms-based strategic vision for the region and its future.

## Transatlantic Trade Dynamics in the Asia-Pacific Region

For both the European Union and the United States, trade has been an essential component of Asia policy. The cornerstone of the Obama administration's Asia rebalance policy has been the conclusion of the comprehensive Trans-Pacific Partnership (TPP) free-trade agreement. The six-year TPP negotiations—which concluded on October 5, 2015—reduce trade barriers with the region's most important economies, including Japan, Australia, New Zealand, Malaysia, and Singapore. Combined, the economic activity conducted by TPP economies amounts to roughly 40 percent of all global trade flows. If passed by the U.S. Congress, TPP will establish a new rules-based policy framework and will provide greater rules-based clarity on emerging trade issues such as digital trade and state-owned enterprises (SOEs), which will benefit U.S. and European consumers and businesses.

---

[14] Wiegand (keynote remarks at "Strengthening EU-U.S. Cooperation in the Asia-Pacific Region" conference).

The TPP is expected to generate more than $295 billion in new economic activity by 2025.[15] It is estimated that the United States would gain short-term economic gains equivalent to 0.5 percent of GDP driven by tariff reductions on critical U.S. exports, particularly agricultural goods and information and communications technologies.[16] With the inclusion of Japan in the accord, the United States will benefit from Tokyo's reduction of (most) tariffs on their top imports such as beef (from 38.5 to 9 percent), dairy (from 40 percent to 0 percent), and wine (from 58 percent to 0 percent).[17] Similarly, Japanese exporters would benefit from reduced barriers on car and auto part sales in the United States. For emerging economies, trade and investment flows generated from TPP will be an important driver of economic growth; the Vietnamese economy is expected to grow by 11 percent over the next 10 years as production operations flow into the country due to its lower labor costs.[18]

The clear economic benefits from TPP are only exceeded by the strengthening of normative standards and international legal commitments. The agreement commits signatories to high labor standards in accordance with the International Labor Organization's fundamental principles, including "collective bargaining rights; prohibitions against child labor and forced labor; requirements for acceptable conditions of work such as minimum wage, hours of work, and safe workplace conditions; and protections against employment discrimination."[19] TPP also guarantees firms recourse in investor-state disputes through an international arbitration mechanism, ensures that SOEs compete with private firms on a level playing field,[20] offers protections to "safeguard U.S. exports and consumers against intellectual property infringement,"[21] reduces barriers to cross-border data flows to facilitate e-commerce, and ensures that the internet remains open.[22]

Despite China's absence from the 12-nation TPP agreement, Beijing will economically benefit from the development of these international trade rules. Indeed, the TPP was designed specifically to be a framework to facilitate the eventual accession of other regional economies—to include China—with the hope that the growth opportunities to be obtained through accession will provide an incentive for countries to conform with TPP's high trade standards. Other significant economies, such as South Korea (which enjoys a bilateral FTA with both the European Union and United States), expressed interest in eventually joining TPP. The participation of the region's largest and most competitive economies in TPP (such as Japan) will ensure that it sets the international standard for other regional trade

---

[15] Larissa A. Brunner, "What Does the TPP Mean for Europe?," *Global Risk Insights*, October 21, 2015, http://globalriskinsights.com/2015/10/what-does-the-tpp-mean-for-europe/.
[16] Peter Petri and Michael Plummer, "The Economic Effects of the Trans-Pacific Partnership: New Estimates," Working Paper no. 16-2, Peterson Institute for International Economics, January 2016, http://www.iie.com/publications/wp/wp16-2.pdf.
[17] Office of the U.S. Trade Representative, "The Trans-Pacific Partnership," fact sheet, n.d., https://ustr.gov/sites/default/files/TPP-Overall-US-Benefits-Fact-Sheet.pdf.
[18] "TPP Trade Deal: Who Stands to Gain, Suffer in Asia-Pacific," Bloomberg, October 6, 2015, http://www.bloomberg.com/news/articles/2015-10-06/tpp-trade-deal-who-stands-to-benefit-suffer-in-asia-pacific.
[19] Office of the U.S. Trade Representative, "The Trans-Pacific Partnership."
[20] Office of the U.S. Trade Representative, "TPP Chapter Summary: State Owned Enterprises (SOEs)," n.d., https://ustr.gov/sites/default/files/TPP-Chapter-Summary-State-Owned-Enterprises.pdf.
[21] Office of the U.S. Trade Representative, "TPP Chapter Summary: Intellectual Property," n.d., https://ustr.gov/sites/default/files/TPP-Chapter-Summary-Intellectual-Property.pdf.
[22] Ibid.

agreements, such as the China-led Regional Comprehensive Economic Partnership (RCEP) talks.

As the broader Doha global trade discussions flagged, the TPP negotiations became a foundational component of a broader, global network of comprehensive regional trade agreements. It was at this moment that Washington should have developed a specific trade coordination mechanism with the European Union as TPP negotiations and the European Union's bilateral free-trade agreements in Asia simultaneously progressed. An early consultation between Washington and Brussels on the U.S.-South Korea FTA and the EU-South Korea trade agreement, for instance, could have developed an appropriate framework for future consultations. Unfortunately, this opportunity was missed. With the inclusion of Japan in TPP, one could imagine that a G7 coordination function could have been formulated to ensure that Western international trade and investment standards would be enshrined in future global trade agreements. Unfortunately, the United States and European Union preferred to remain as trade competitors in Asia rather than partners.

However, there is another critical transatlantic opportunity for consultation that should not be missed: coordination between the EU-China comprehensive investment agreement and the U.S.-China Bilateral Investment Treaty (BIT). While transatlantic trade negotiators have exchanged views, it would be valuable to have either a formal G7 or U.S.-EU consultation as these parallel negotiations with Beijing take place. If yet another trade coordination opportunity is missed, the United States and European Union could find themselves working against each other and not in support of unified international trade standards.

After nearly six years of economic stagnation, the European Union has made its foreign trade agenda an essential component of its policy in an effort to attract foreign investment, obtain greater access to export markets, and stimulate growth. Since the collapse of EU-ASEAN free-trade talks in 2009 (primarily due to concerns over Myanmar's human rights track record), Brussels has pursued bilateral free-trade agreements with several East and Southeast Asian economies that would eventually serve as "the building blocks towards a future region-to-region agreement.[23] In 2010 the European Union launched FTA negotiations with Thailand and Malaysia, and has finalized agreements with Singapore (October 2014) and Vietnam (December 2015). ASEAN is now the European Union's third-largest trading partner, and trade with Europe totaled 13 percent of ASEAN trade in 2013.[24] More than 10,000 European businesses now conduct operations in the Asia-Pacific region.[25] Further, 22 percent of all inbound foreign direct investment (FDI) into ASEAN originates from the 28 nations of European Union. Beyond ASEAN, Brussels also concluded an FTA with South Korea in October 2010 and is reprioritizing its free-trade agreement negotiations with Tokyo.

---

[23] High Representative of the Union for Foreign Affairs and Security Policy, "Joint Communication to the European Parliament and the Council: The EU and ASEAN: A Partnership with a Strategic Purpose," European Commission, May 18, 2015, http://eur-lex.europa.eu/legal-content/EN/TXT/PDF/?uri=JOIN:2015:22:FIN&from=EN.
[24] European Commission, "Trade: Countries and regions: Association of South East Asian Nations (ASEAN)," 2014, http://ec.europa.eu/trade/policy/countries-and-regions/regions/asean/.
[25] Ji Xianbai, "Time to Revisit an ASEAN-EU FTA?," *The Diplomat*, June 3, 2015, http://thediplomat.com/2015/06/time-to-revisit-an-asean-eu-fta/.

As direct result of TPP, the European Union is projected to lose between -0.02 to -0.1 percent of GDP growth annually due to trade diversion.[26] Although the overall impact is relatively muted, the consequences will be more significant for certain sectors and industries that have deeply entrenched interests in Asia. The European (and specifically, German) auto industry, for instance, would experience a reduction in its share of global value added by -1.48 percent as a direct consequence of a comprehensive TPP agreement coming into effect, which would correspond to a reduction in incomes in countries that are closely integrated into the German supply chain.[27] If TPP is expanded to include other key EU export markets (such as South Korea, Indonesia, or even China), this impact may become even more pronounced at a time when Europe's recovery has lagged in part due to weak demand for manufactured goods.

Perhaps more detrimental, however, is the impact that TPP will have on Europe's ability to advance its own trade agenda in the absence of a preexisting transatlantic consensus on trade and investment standards. Although the transatlantic economy is already one of the most closely integrated in the world and Europe will benefit from many of the architectural enhancements from TPP by default, Washington and Brussels maintain different positions on several controversial issues such as data protection, state procurement policies, genetically modified organisms (GMOs), geographic indicators (GIs), and investor-state dispute settlement (ISDS). This reality not only has slowed progress on the U.S.-EU Transatlantic Trade and Investment Partnership (TTIP) talks but could complicate the establishment of new international trade and investment standards and their universal application in Asia. As Asian partners increasingly point to TPP as a template, Europeans leaders may not be prepared to accept U.S. trade and investment standards in these sensitive areas. As Dutch Prime Minister Mark Rutte has stated, the "TPP deal can't simply be copied and pasted" into other agreements.[28]

Consequently, Europeans have grown increasingly concerned that TPP reduces their future bargaining power in trade talks. EU-Japanese negotiations, for example, have understandably slowed because of Tokyo's focus on completing its TPP negotiations. But Tokyo has resisted European calls for protection of geographic indicators and the maintenance of certain agricultural tariffs (such as on pork and cereal). The Japanese government also has made it clear that its preference is for the more widely accepted (U.S.-supported) investor-state dispute settlement (ISDS) mechanism and not an independent or "reformed" ISDS that the European Union has proposed. On the other hand, the EU-Vietnam FTA establishes an independent ISDS tribunal under the terms of the accord. Will the United States' or European Union's trade preferences in Asia win out or will there be a patchwork of agreements, underscoring the lack of transatlantic unity?

---

[26] Marek Wasinski, "Europe Left Behind: Trans-Pacific Partnership and Its Impact on the EU," Bulletin No. 92 (824), Polish Institute of International Affairs (PISM), October 19, 2015, https://www.pism.pl/files/?id_plik=20683.
[27] Rahel Aichele and Gabriel Felbermayr, "The Trans-Pacific Partnership Deal (TPP): What are the economic consequences for in- and outsiders?," GED (Global Economic Dynamics) Focus Paper, Bertelsmann Stiftung, October 8, 2015, https://www.bertelsmann-stiftung.de/fileadmin/files/BSt/Publikationen/GrauePublikationen/Economic_Effects_of_TPP_IFO_GED.pdf.
[28] Loreline Merelle, "Dutch PM Seeks Ambitious EU-Japan FTA That Is Not a Copy of TPP," *Japan Times*, November 7, 2015, http://www.japantimes.co.jp/news/2015/11/07/national/politics-diplomacy/dutch-pm-seeks-ambitious-eu-japan-fta-that-is-not-a-copy-of-tpp/#.Vuxe0-IrIdV.

As TPP consolidates its position in Asia's trade architecture, the European Union has accelerated and expanded its FTA initiatives in Asia in response. In October 2015, EU trade commissioner Cecilia Malmström indicated that the European Union would reevaluate whether or not to resume FTA talks with ASEAN in light of the democratic transition occurring in Myanmar as well as the bloc's decision to formally create a single, economic market in Southeast Asia. The commission has also announced that it will pursue trade talks with New Zealand, Australia, and the Philippines, but it will likely be several years before these agreements are finalized—meaning that TPP will continue to influence trade relations in Asia.

Taking stock of the evolving trade dynamics in the Asia Pacific, the lack of coordination between the United States and Europe has created an environment where the United States and European Union are more competitors than partners but where both sides miss important opportunities to advance the international rules and normative behavior that both support. While the United States and its TPP partners have largely set the tone for EU trade negotiations in Asia (absent China), Europe is seeking to balance this advantage with greater economic cooperation with China. So, a choice must be taken by both sides of the Atlantic: to pursue separate interests that will likely undercut the policy work of the other (which Asian partners will exploit to their advantage) or work together on a future-looking global trade framework. If the European Union continues to pursue independent trade agreements in the Asia Pacific, critical components of these accords will likely be incompatible with TPP— thereby undermining Washington's strategic global trade vision, and vice versa.

## Transatlantic Divergence on Market Economy Status for China

The inability of the European Union and United States to effectively coordinate their strategic agendas in the Asia-Pacific region is most apparent over their respective policies toward China. Although it is important to note that China is not Asia and engagement with regional partners is of equal importance, China is a country toward which transatlantic policy coordination is most needed and where it seems most elusive. China's recent military activism in East Asia, particularly in relation to its maritime disputes with its neighbors in the South and East China Seas, has produced an increasingly unstable regional security environment in which Beijing has violated international law (this issue will be discussed in greater detail in the next chapter).

Responding to these violations is where transatlantic policy divergences have emerged most clearly. The EU view that it is not a geopolitical actor in Asia permits it to approach China solely through an economic and trade lens, whereas the United States—as a geopolitical actor—views China's maritime activities as infringing on international laws. The United States wants to see China successfully emerge as a responsible and engaged global partner in its foreign, security, and economic policies, yet China's economic strength cannot be separated from its violations of international law in the South and East China Seas. When international rules are violated, costs must be imposed on states, large and small. This is not geopolitical; it is the sanctity of international law and international standards. China's growing economic power can be a force for positive regional development or it can be used as a negative or malign instrument. Both the United States and European Union have important equities in Asia's regional stability. Without stability, there cannot be economic growth.

The transatlantic policy divergence between several EU member states and the United States over participation in the AIIB was one of the most visible policy divergences witnessed in the region, but unfortunately "there will be other AIIBs." The most significant will be the granting of Market Economic Status (MES). By the end of 2016, the European Union will decide whether or not to grant China MES per the terms of China's WTO accession agreement. Conferring China with MES would make it much harder for the European Union to apply trade protections against Chinese exports, which could allow Beijing to unfairly dump its excess industrial capacity (particularly steel) on European markets at the expense of European producers. Chinese officials, appealing to Europe's desire to respect international agreements, have ironically called on the European Union to deliver a positive response "as an important member of the WTO and important supporting force of international rule of law in the multilateral trade system...."[29] The United States, however, does not believe that China has earned this status due to its reluctance to fully comply with WTO standards as evidenced by Beijing's frequent intervention in its economy.

In June 2015, EU lawyers opined in a confidential assessment that "it would be unwise not to grant market-economy treatment towards China."[30] But EU member states are split on the issue depending on their economic interests vis-à-vis China and the harm that could be done to their economies absent the continuation of adequate antidumping protections. The European Union is currently undertaking a comprehensive impact assessment and conducting stakeholder outreach in order to understand what granting China MES would mean for the EU economy—particularly with regard to sensitive industries (such as steel, textiles, and solar panels) in which China continues to overproduce, allowing it to sell its goods cheaply in foreign markets. Some economists have estimated that there could be a 1 to 2 percent reduction in EU GDP should MES be granted, likely raising unemployment at a time when the European average rate is still in double digits—making the debate highly sensitive at a volatile moment in European politics.[31] In this climate, EU trade commissioner Cecilia Malmström, speaking in Washington, made clear that, regardless of the final decision on MES, China would need to "behave responsibly" and would be subject to duties if it failed to do so.[32]

The MES decision is ultimately up to EU institutions, the European Parliament, and member states.[33] However, the MES issue will profoundly shape future transatlantic relations vis-a-vis China and the Asia-Pacific region. If the transatlantic community learned one thing from the debacle over the AIIB it was that, as in all things, transatlantic policy unity toward this region is vital. The United States and the European Union are fierce trade and investment competitors but both partners are also keenly interested in defending and defining the

---

[29] David Lawder, "Update 2-EU to Keep Strong Trade Defences Even with China Shift—official," CNBC, March 10, 2016, http://www.cnbc.com/2016/03/10/reuters-america-update-2-eu-to-keep-strong-trade-defences-even-with-china-shift-official.html.
[30] Matthew Dalton, "EU Lawyers Favor Market-Economy Status for China Next Year," *Wall Street Journal*, June 9, 2015, http://www.wsj.com/articles/eu-lawyers-favor-market-economy-status-for-china-next-year-1433873355.
[31] Robert Scott and Xiao Jiang, "Unilateral Grant of Market Economy Status to China Would Put Millions of EU Jobs at Risk," Economic Policy Institute, September 18, 2015, http://www.epi.org/publication/eu-jobs-at-risk/.
[32] Lawder, "Update 2-EU to Keep Strong Trade Defences Even with China Shift—official."
[33] Eszter Zalan, "Divided EU debates China market economy status," *EU Observer*, January 13, 2016, https://euobserver.com/eu-china/131801.

highest international trade standards and legal norms. Too often, there have been lost opportunities to uphold and promote these values in Asia.

## Recommendations for Strengthening EU-U.S. Economic Cooperation in Asia

- *Create a Structured Dialogue Regarding China's Market Economy Status (MES).* Greater policy prioritization and urgency must be given to the creation of a U.S.-EU structured dialogue to consult over granting MES to China. In 2015, European and U.S. trade negotiators met for consultations over the U.S.-China BIT and EU-China comprehensive investment agreements.[34] In the future, these conversations should be expanded to include China's MES. If agreement cannot be reached over MES, the European Union and United States must work together to ensure there is an agreed process for addressing policy difference.

- *Develop a Joint Vision for Trade Policies in Emerging Sectors.* The U.S. and EU trade negotiators should identify and then develop a roadmap for areas where international trade rules are scarce. To develop international trade and investment policies for these new trade spaces, a comparative analysis of TPP and bilateral EU FTAs should be undertaken to identify the early emergence of agreed-upon norms. This will be particularly important for standards related to IT.

- *Prioritize Dialogue on Asian Economics at the G7 Summit.* As a leading economic forum that brings together the United States, European Union, and Japan, the G7 is a natural arena to deepen and enhance EU-U.S. economic cooperation in the region. Informal consultations related to the evolving economic dynamics of and trade patterns related to the Asia-Pacific region should be consistently on the G7 Summit agenda to ensure effective coordination on international practices and standards.

- *Establish a Transatlantic Dialogue on ASEAN Connectivity.* Consideration should be given to developing a dedicated consultative mechanism related to EU and U.S. initiatives on enhancing ASEAN's connectivity and infrastructure to avoid duplication and to ensure the highest international trade and investment standards.

- *Trilateralize Transatlantic Consultations with ASEAN.* Consideration should also be given to developing a trilateral U.S.-EU-ASEAN consultation on an annual basis. Already, the United States and the European Union meet with their ASEAN partners at forums, yet the European Union and United States do not jointly participate in these sessions. A new forum would help to reinforce transatlantic unity in the region, while helping to facilitate the development of a mutual agenda in areas where policy interests converge, and thereby enable ASEAN to play a more central role in the Asian economic architecture.

---

[34] Scott Miller (remarks at "Strengthening EU-U.S. Cooperation in the Asia-Pacific Region" conference, CSIS, Washington, DC, February 17, 2016), http://csis.org/multimedia/audio-strengthening-eu-us-cooperation-asia-pacific-region.

# 02

# Developing a Transatlantic Vision for Asia-Pacific Security Cooperation

## Introduction

The United States and the European Union share a common foreign and security policy vision for the Asia-Pacific region: to uphold peace and stability, to ensure respect for international law, principles, and institutions, and to safeguard the unimpeded flow of commerce in maritime Asia. This vital region, however, is far from stable. In Northeast Asia, North Korea represents a real and growing threat as it defies United Nations sanctions and continues to develop nuclear weapons and intercontinental ballistic missiles capable of delivering them. In Southeast Asia, there are growing tensions between China (which seeks to create maritime features and turn them into military outposts and frequently harasses neighboring states' vessels, ships, and fishermen) and the other littoral Southeast Asian states.

As a dynamic and growing economic area, the Asia-Pacific region contains some of the world's most critical sea lines of communication (SLOC). The overlapping maritime claims in the South China Sea, an expanse of waters through which $5 trillion worth of trade passes each year, have emerged as a new security flashpoint in East Asia and will remain contested between China and five Southeast Asian countries—Brunei, Indonesia, Malaysia, the Philippines, and Vietnam—for the foreseeable future (Taiwan also lays claim to certain features, although it is prohibited from pursuing them due to its international status). The waters surrounding the Strait of Malacca—the world's second-most-important strategic chokepoint in terms of volume of oil transit[35]—have also reemerged as a hotspot of piracy attacks, accounting for over half of the world's reported piracy and armed robbery incidents in 2015.[36] These waters are also a source of illegal fishing, weapons proliferation, migration, and environmental challenges. The growing interest and involvement of the international community in the territorial and maritime disputes as well as environmental issues in the South China Sea may internationalize these regional and balance-of-power politics in the coming years.

In the East China Sea, the dispute over the sovereignty of Senkaku Islands—claimed by both China (referred to as the Diaoyu Islands) and Japan but administered by Japan—continues to be a source of tension in relations between the second- and third-largest economies in the

---

[35] U.S. Energy Information Administration (EIA), "World Oil Transit Chokepoints," https://www.eia.gov/beta/international/regions-topics.cfm?RegionTopicID=WOTC.

[36] Commercial Crime Services, "IMB: Maritime Piracy Hotspots Persist Worldwide despite Reductions in Key Areas," February 2, 2016, https://icc-ccs.org/news/1154-imb-maritime-piracy-hotspots-persist-worldwide-despite-reductions-in-key-areas.

world. Concerns about China's increased military activities in the region have prompted the Japanese government to rethink its decades-long pacifist posture of its Self Defense Forces and expand its security resources both at home and across the region. The United States, Japan's longstanding ally, has reaffirmed its commitment to come to Tokyo's defense should Japanese control of the Senkaku Islands come under threat, although Washington officially does not take sides in the sovereignty dispute.[37] In a joint statement with Japanese Prime Minister Abe, President Obama noted that the United States' "treaty commitment to Japan's security is absolute, and that Article 5 [of the U.S.-Japan Treaty] covers all territories under Japan's administration, including the Senkaku Islands."

Across the region, international norms and rules are increasingly being challenged, which has had a destabilizing effect on the region. If states neither enforce international rules nor impose costs on violations of international law, an international policy vacuum will emerge in which states can take advantage of perceived weakness and pursue their own policy goals. For the United States, a failure to uphold its commitments in the Asia Pacific would come at the expense of the international legal system and its closest allies and trading partners, as well as constitute a dramatic loss of credibility and reputational damage. While the European Union may feel distant and indifferent to security developments in East Asia due to its geography, the outcomes of these developments will reverberate globally. Thus, both the United States and European Union have a strategic imperative to ensure that international norms and values are managed and upheld in the security sphere, and it is in their mutual interest to work together to maintain and reinforce Asia's emerging security architecture.

## U.S. Security Posture in the Asia-Pacific Region

For decades, the United States has maintained robust permanent military and naval deployments throughout the Asia Pacific and has continued to prioritize them in the face of budgetary constraints. Above all, U.S. force posture in the Western Pacific is intended to reinforce America's treaty obligations and develop a durable Asian security architecture. In May 2015 at the Shangri-La Dialogue in Singapore, U.S. Defense Secretary Ash Carter stated that "the United States wants a shared regional architecture that is strong enough, capable enough, and connected enough to ensure that all Asia-Pacific peoples and nations have the opportunity to rise and continue to rise in the future."[38] The United States now embraces a more proactive security approach toward the region that is designed to confront the region's "increasingly fraught" security environment.

Washington's presence is strongest in Northeast Asia, in large part due to Pyongyang's continued violation of United Nations Security Council resolutions and continued bellicosity. In Japan and South Korea combined, the United States has stationed more than 15,000 marines, 20,000 ground troops, over 20,000 air force personnel, and close to 20,000 navy

---

[37] Office of the Press Secretary, "Joint Press Conference with President Obama and Prime Minister Abe of Japan," White House, April 24, 2014, https://www.whitehouse.gov/the-press-office/2014/04/24/joint-press-conference-president-obama-and-prime-minister-abe-japan.
[38] Tyrone C. Marshall Jr., "Carter: Asia-Pacific Will Continue to 'Rise' With Strong Security Architecture," *Defense News*, May 30, 2015, http://www.defense.gov/News-Article-View/Article/604750/carter-asia-pacific-will-continue-to-rise-with-strong-security-architecture.

sailors.[39] Despite intense international pressure over the last two decades, North Korea has continued to pursue its development of a nuclear weapon arsenal while developing ICBM capabilities that could reach the United States. Pyongyang's repeated nuclear tests (some of which have reportedly been successful) and bellicose rhetoric have led to an expansion of UN sanctions, but do not appear to dissuade North Korean leader Kim Jung-un from his singular mission. North Korea's actions have led the United States to consider the deployment of a terminal high-altitude area missile defense system (THAAD) to South Korea in the future, as well as an increased military presence in the region.

Beijing's escalating regional military posture, assertiveness toward its neighbors, and perceived challenges to international maritime norms have also caused the United States to begin enhancing its military presence in Southeast Asia. Above all, Washington seeks to ensure the preservation of peace and stability, uphold international laws and norms in the region, and guarantee freedom of navigation in the lucrative waters of East Asia. The Pentagon has reached agreements to station rotational forces in the Philippines, Australia, and Singapore, and is working with other regional partners to enhance defense and naval cooperation.[40] Singapore will also host four U.S. combat ships, and Vietnam has stepped up its military engagement with Washington through regular noncombat exercises (the United States has also agreed to partially lift its longstanding arms embargo against Vietnam).

Washington has also recently embraced a more proactive policy approach toward the South China Sea as U.S. officials increasingly see China's expansionist policies and disregard for its maritime neighbors as detrimental to the international legal order and rules-based institutions and regimes. The United States has initiated freedom-of-navigation operations (FONOPs) to assert its international maritime rights. In October 2015 the United States controversially conducted these operations within the 12-nautical-mile radius surrounding artificial Chinese structures in the South China Sea for the first time. Although the maneuver was not intended to challenge Chinese sovereignty, it was designed to reinforce that the United States does not recognize the legal entitlements of these man-made features.[41] Also in 2015, the United States announced a Southeast Asia Maritime Security Initiative to improve regional maritime domain awareness. Activities include law enforcement support as well as improvements to intelligence, surveillance, and reconnaissance (ISR) and command and control capabilities.

The United States has sought the engagement of its European allies to help strengthen the international legal and institutional regime in Southeast Asia, and in particular with ASEAN. The European Union is also interested in strengthening Southeast Asian nations' capacity building and preparedness in humanitarian assistance and disaster relief (HA/DR) response, the ability to address threats posed by nontraditional maritime security challenges (e.g.,

---

[39] Asia Maritime Transparency Initiative (AMTI), "18 Maps That Explain Maritime Security in Asia: U.S. Military Personnel in East Asia," CSIS, 2014, http://amti.csis.org/atlas/.

[40] Ernest Z. Bower, Murray Hiebert, Phuong Nguyen, and Gregory B. Poling, *Southeast Asia's Geopolitical Centrality and the U.S.-Japan Alliance* (Washington, DC: CSIS, June 2015), http://csis.org/files/publication/150609_Bower_SoutheastAsiaCentrality_Web.pdf.

[41] Michael J. Green, Bonnie S. Glaser, and Gregory B. Poling, "The U.S. Asserts Freedom of Navigation in the South China Sea," *CSIS Critical Questions*, October 27, 2015, http://csis.org/publication/us-asserts-freedom-navigation-south-china-sea.

maritime piracy, marine environmental protection), freedom of navigation and overflight, and the peaceful resolution of disputes through noncoercive means. Despite a shared vision and economic benefits, however, the European Union and the United States have not always acted in concert to jointly defend these common interests.

## EU Perspectives on Security in the Asia-Pacific Region

The European Union has stated that:

> Asia is of strategic and security importance for the European Union. Therefore, the EU's relationship with Asia has become more comprehensive, expanding from its initial focus on economic and trade matters to encompass the political, strategic and security dimension. As a provider of peace and stability in Europe through effective multilateralism and integration, the EU is supporting the building of a security architecture in Asia to address and manage the various security challenges. . . . [by] (1) Establishing the EU as a credible political and security player in the region through demonstrating relevant expertise and working with key allies from inside and outside the region. (2) Supporting the region to manage security challenges for example through helping to build an effective regional security architecture with ASEAN at the centre and through providing technical assistance. (3) Working with the region to confront shared regional and global security challenges.[42]

Yet, despite this commitment EU funding has largely been devoted to development assistance and trade facilitation. For example, the European Union will provide ASEAN with €170 million in funding between 2014 and 2020 to "enhance connectivity/trade, address disaster management/climate change and promote dialogue across the board."[43] It will also provide nearly €2 billion in direct bilateral development aid to individual ASEAN members. None of this funding is specifically earmarked for defense and security partnerships.

However, the joint statement issued in July 2012 by U.S. secretary of state Hillary Clinton and EU high representative Catherine Ashton in Phnom Penh was an important first step to engaging the European Union in supporting international legal norms (and therefore regional security and stability in Southeast Asia), as well as to help push the reform process and democratic opening in Myanmar forward in 2011–2012.[44] The EU-U.S. statement committed both sides to "work with Asian partners on increasing maritime security based on international law as reflected in the United Nations Convention on the Law of the Sea (UNCLOS), and lend assistance to the development of confidence building measures to reduce the risk of crises and conflict."[45] With regards to the South China Sea, the statement

---

[42] European External Action Service, "EU-Asia Security," fact sheet, May 26, 2013, http://eeas.europa.eu/asia/docs/eu_in_asia_factsheet_en.pdf.

[43] European Union External Action Service, "The European Union and the Association of Southeast Asian Nations: Towards an Ever Stronger Natural Partnership," fact sheet, July 22, 2014, http://www.eeas.europa.eu/statements/docs/2014/140722_03_en.pdf.

[44] Office of the Spokesperson, "U.S.-EU Statement on the Asia-Pacific Region," U.S. Department of State, media note, July 12, 2012, http://www.state.gov/r/pa/prs/ps/2012/07/194896.htm.

[45] Ibid.

urges ASEAN and China to work toward a code of conduct and resolve maritime and territorial disputes through diplomatic, peaceful, and cooperative means.[46]

In practice, however, European countries' interest in maritime security developments in the region has not gone beyond diplomatic statements. While the European Union shares U.S. objectives on maritime security in the Asia Pacific and is in the process of including a security dimension to its engagement with the region, the European Union possesses limited overseas projection capabilities such as available active aircraft carriers. Beyond continued engagement by former colonial powers such as the United Kingdom and France, the European Union does not view itself as a geopolitical actor in Asia, but it is a beneficiary of the U.S. naval presence and open sea lines in the South China Sea. Given declining European defense spending and a limited ability to project conventional military forces in Asia,[47] Europe has largely been a security free-rider in Asia even as major EU countries expand economic and diplomatic engagement. Moreover, unlike the United States, European countries do not possess a network of bilateral treaty alliances with Asian countries, which limits both Europe's level of strategic engagement with the region and its appreciation of geopolitical dynamics there. The European External Action Service (EEAS) managing director for the Asia-Pacific region recently amplified this message by stating that the European Union's agenda in Asia is not geopolitical.[48]

But the policy voice of the 28-country European Union does carry significant reputational weight when it is used, particularly in concert with the United States, on international legal norms despite the European Union's reluctance to speak out about violations of international law in the Asia-Pacific region, particularly as many unavoidably touch on the regional behavior and role of China. The European Union hesitates to use its public bully pulpit, fearing Beijing's potential use of economic and political isolation or punishment, and therefore couches its public statements as being perceived as "sometimes useful and sometimes counter-productive."[49]

U.S. officials believe, however, that a more public and forward-leaning approach by the European Union would make clear that transatlantic allies are of one mind when it comes to backing international legal principles such as UNCLOS, respect for the peaceful settlement of disputes, and the upholding of freedom of navigation and overflight by all parties.[50] The European Union has too often chosen a quiet and cautious approach to the region's maritime disputes, preferring that European leaders' words and actions not contribute to existing tensions among key players in the South China Sea. This is why the recent message by the EU high representative related the South China Sea is particularly welcome and seen as an important first step for the European Union to take a more vocal and active role in

---

[46] Ibid.
[47] Phillip C. Saunders, "The Strategic Logic of the U.S. Rebalance to Asia and a Potential European Role," German Marshall Fund Policy Brief, June 11, 2013, http://www.gmfus.org/publications/strategic-logic-us-rebalance-asia-and-potential-european-role.
[48] Wiegand (keynote remarks at "Strengthening EU-U.S. Cooperation in the Asia-Pacific Region" conference).
[49] David Brunnstrom and Idrees Ali, "U.S. Says Europeans Could Help More in South Sea Dispute," Reuters, July 19, 2015, http://www.reuters.com/article/us-usa-eu-southchinasea-idUSKCN0Q401B20150730.
[50] Ibid.

defending international legal norms.[51] Although brief, the statement clearly states that "the EU is committed to maintaining a legal order for the seas and oceans based on the principles of international law," and "urges all claimants to resolve disputes through peaceful means" and "to refrain from militarization . . . or the use or threat of force."

## Role and Implications of EU Members' Security Partnerships in the Asia-Pacific Region

Because developments affecting maritime security in the region have often been secondary to EU countries' economic priorities in Asia and their increasing interest in reaching new markets (particularly in Southeast Asia), enhancing EU-U.S. security cooperation in Asia has not been fully explored. Unfortunately, U.S. and EU officials also have not effectively built on the momentum of general transatlantic cooperation in Asia that was cemented during the early days of the U.S. rebalance to Asia, which culminated in the joint Clinton-Ashton ASEAN statement in 2012.

To the extent that European countries have shown an interest in maritime security trends in Asia, it is the United Kingdom that has been the most outspoken about its support for the principles of international law in accordance with UNCLOS, peaceful dispute settlement, and free and lawful use of the world's oceans.[52] The UK has longstanding historical, business, people-to-people, and defense links with Malaysia, Brunei, and Singapore—as former British colonies and protectorates—which provides a unique platform to reach out to neighboring Southeast Asian countries. The UK's security cooperation with Malaysia and Singapore encompasses joint military training and intelligence sharing. The UK has also sought to develop greater bilateral cooperation with Indonesia on maritime, defense, and space technology, and has increased its defense industrial, military training, and maritime cooperation with Vietnam.[53] British Prime Minister David Cameron's 2015 visit to Southeast Asia was an important strategic engagement of and high-level exchanges by an EU member with Asia since the 2012 joint U.S.-EU statement.

The British as well as the French navy pay regular port calls to facilities in Singapore and Malaysia, and have conducted humanitarian assistance/disaster relief exchanges as well as naval exercises with regional forces including the Japanese Maritime Self-Defense Force, the Republic of Korea Navy, the Malaysian Armed Forces, and the U.S. Navy in the Asia-Pacific theater. For example, the Royal Navy quickly deployed the HMS *Daring* and HMS *Illustrious* to take part in the multinational HA/DR effort in the aftermath of Typhoon Haiyan in the

---

[51] Council of the European Union, "Declaration by the High Representative on behalf of the EU on Recent Developments in the South China Sea," press release, March 11, 2016, http://www.consilium.europa.eu/en/press/press-releases/2016/03/11-hr-declaration-on-bealf-of-eu-recent-developments-south-china-sea/.

[52] British Embassy Hanoi, "Joint Statement by the UK and Vietnam on UK Prime Minister's Visit to Vietnam," news release, July 30, 2015, https://www.gov.uk/government/world-location-news/joint-statement-by-the-uk-and-vietnam-on-uk-prime-ministers-visit-to-vietnam.

[53] Rui Hao Puah, "The United Kingdom Needs Sustained Engagement with Southeast Asia," *CogitAsia* (blog), CSIS, August 17, 2015, http://cogitasia.com/the-united-kingdom-needs-sustained-engagement-with-southeast-asia/.

Philippines in November 2013 [54]—the HMS *Daring* was at the time on a nine-month deployment to the Asia-Pacific region.[55] The French Navy maintains more than 4,000 troops prepositioned in French overseas territories in the Pacific and Indian Oceans, including French Polynesia, New Caledonia, and Réunion Island, accounting for over 30 percent of French forces deployed overseas. French forces prepositioned in New Caledonia and French Polynesia took part in rescue and disaster relief efforts following Tropical Cyclone Pam in Vanuatu in March 2015.[56]

It is also important to note that three EU members (France, United Kingdom, Netherlands) and NATO member Norway participated in the 2014 RIMPAC exercises—clearly demonstrating that a diverse range of European allies are growing increasingly concerned about instability in the Asia-Pacific region. In total, 49 warships, 6 submarines, 200 aircraft, and 25,000 personnel from all 22 contributing nations participated in the month-long exercises, which provided an important opportunity for EU and NATO members to gain valuable experience conducting maritime operations with their Asian partners and allies.[57]

With two of the European Union's most militarily advanced member states engaged in a security partnership in the Asia-Pacific region, securing a more robust EU position on Asian security is achievable given the rapid changes in the South China Sea, but it will require more intense diplomatic efforts and coordination.

## Identifying New Opportunities to Strengthen EU-U.S. Cooperation in Asia-Pacific Maritime Security

The following suggests several opportunities to strengthen U.S.-EU security cooperation in the Asia-Pacific region.

- *Prepare a Joint Statement on the Outcome of the Tribunal of the Permanent Arbitration Court in The Hague.* An important and fast-approaching opportunity is for the European Union and the United States to issue a joint statement following the ruling of the Arbitral Tribunal in The Hague, where the Philippines has challenged Beijing's maritime entitlements (nine-dash line) and claims in the South China Sea. Although Beijing does not accept the jurisdiction of the Arbitral Tribunal, a ruling in support of the Philippines could be an opportunity to strengthen international legal norms and highlight for China the increased international reputational risks of maintaining a position that is not accepted by its main trading partners. Preparations should also be made in the event the ruling does not clearly favor one side or the

---

[54] UK Royal Navy, "Operation Patwin," http://www.royalnavy.mod.uk/news-and-latest-activity/operations/pacific/patwin.
[55] UK Royal Navy, "HMS *Daring* Goes Global," news release, May 15, 2013, http://www.royalnavy.mod.uk/news-and-latest-activity/news/2013/may/15/130515-hms-daring-goes-global.
[56] Kelvin Wong, "France Flexes Asia-Pacific HADR and Power-Projection Capabilities with Latest Jeanne d'Arc Deployment," *IHS Jane's Defence Weekly*, April 27, 2015, http://www.janes.com/article/50984/france-flexes-asia-pacific-hadr-and-power-projection-capabilities-with-latest-jeanne-d-arc-deployment.
[57] SHAPE (Supreme Headquarters Allied Powers Europe) Public Affairs Office, "NATO participates in largest international maritime exercise: RIMPAC 2014," July 23, 2014, https://www.shape.nato.int/nato-participates-in-largest-international-maritime-exercise-rimpac-2014.

other. A joint EU-U.S. statement must affirm international legal principles. There have been early warning signs that the United States and Europe are not on the same page. At the end of 2015 shortly following the visit of Chinese president Xi Jinping, the United Kingdom sought to obtain the status of "neutral observer" in the Philippine tribunal at the Permanent Court of Arbitration, a decision that reportedly took U.S. and Philippine officials by surprise and prompted concerns that London's request was intended to assist Beijing to monitor developments in the case.[58] British officials have noted that the request was a routine intervention in international maritime affairs. The United States was denied observer status due to a lack of territorial involvement in the dispute. Again, confusion stemming from a lack of communication and policy coordination can easily be misinterpreted, as we have too often seen with regard to the United States and European Union in Asia.

- *Initiate a Renewed EU-U.S. Diplomatic Push for the Completion of a Maritime Code of Conduct.* Following the Arbitral Tribunal ruling, the United States and European Union, with ASEAN members, should revitalize the pursuit of a code of conduct. There could also be an effort to create a "Vientiane Declaration" (Laos chairs ASEAN in 2016) along the lines of the 2008 Ilulissat Declaration (in which the five Arctic littoral states agreed to abide by UNCLOS as the international legal governing framework for the Arctic) for the South China Sea coastal states to reconfirm that the international legal framework in the region is based on UNCLOS and to support the rapid adoption of a code of conduct.

- *Increase the Number of European Countries Participating in the 2016 RIMPAC Exercises.* In June and July 2016, the U.S. Pacific Command will host the 25th installment of the RIMPAC exercises. While four European allies (of which three are EU members) participated in the last round, several European naval powers—including Germany, Italy, and Spain—were absent. Broadening European participation in Pacific exercises will not only help to enhance naval cooperation between European countries and their Asian partners, but send a strong signal that the European Union has a strong interest in seeing that freedom of navigation is upheld in the region—and that EU members are willing to commit resources to enforce it. It is anticipated that China will participate for the second consecutive round as well.

- *Initiate an EU-U.S. Costs Imposition Consultation in Response to Violations of International Law.* Should violations of international maritime law continue and if maritime disputes are settled by force in the South China Sea, there should be a discussion of joint efforts to impose costs on the parties that violate international law.

- *Consider Trilateralizing EU-U.S.-ASEAN Cooperation on an International Rules-Based Approach.* EU interlocutors should be invited as observers to U.S.-ASEAN meetings with participation in supporting the development of regional institutional architecture and strengthening legal norms.

---

[58] Owen Bowcott, "UK requests observer status in legal dispute over South China Sea islands," *The Guardian*, November 25, 2015, http://www.theguardian.com/politics/2015/nov/25/uk-requests-observer-status-spratly-islands-dispute.

- *Create a Permanent Asia-Pacific Consultation at the G7 Leaders Level.* The members of the Group of Seven should create a permanent agenda item related to political, economic, and security developments in the Asia-Pacific region to develop shared understanding and shared solutions. As Japan currently chairs the G7, this effort would be ideally launched during the upcoming May 2016 G7 Summit.

- *Expand European Participation in Southeast Asian Antipiracy Efforts.* As Southeast Asian maritime security has come under increased threat from pirates and illicit trafficking, both the United States and European Union possess the know-how and resources to help the region combat piracy. Indeed, one of the most successful examples of transatlantic security cooperation is the joint antipiracy campaign (Operation Atalanta) in the Horn of Africa and Indian Ocean. Once a hotbed of illegal activity, in 2015 there were no illegal attacks in waters patrolled by EU forces.[59] Already, the United States and several European partners (the United Kingdom, Denmark, Norway, and the Netherlands) participate in the Japanese-led Regional Cooperation Agreement on Combating Piracy and Armed Robbery against Ships in Asia (ReCAAP), and EU membership would provide an opportunity for Brussels to share its valuable expertise and enhance its contribution to Asian maritime security. China and South Korea have participated in Operation Atalanta, setting a precedent for multilateral engagement.

- *Consider European Membership of the Expanded ASEAN Maritime Forum.* In 2012, ASEAN launched the Expanded ASEAN Maritime Forum, which brings together government and nongovernment representatives from the countries participating in the East Asia Summit (EAS) to emphasize collaboration on improving maritime domain awareness; share best practices, maritime connectivity, and capacity building; and encourage the rule of law at sea. While the United States currently participates in this dialogue, there is presently no European participation. This forum could invite European nations, such as the United Kingdom and France, which have considerable equities in Southeast Asia, to participate as observers.

---

[59] Paul Richardson, "Piracy Threat Rises for Ships off Somalia This Year, IHS Says," Bloomberg, January 25, 2016, http://www.bloomberg.com/news/articles/2016-01-25/piracy-threat-rises-for-ships-off-somalia-this-year-ihs-says.

# 03

# Conclusion

The European Union and the United States have both rebalanced their policies toward Asia and share mutual economic and security interests in the region. Both stand to gain by ensuring that the region's institutional architecture is strengthened in the economic and security spheres and that the Asia-Pacific region remains stable, predictable, peaceful, and conducive to trade and investment. The United States and European Union possess enormous resources, expertise, and capacity that can be applied in pursuit of these goals. Unfortunately in the Asia-Pacific region, Washington and Brussels have not always looked to each other to jointly pursue these mutually beneficial regional and international rules-based objectives. Rather, the European Union and United States have pursued separate policies and independent agendas in the region that have, on occasion, run contrary to each other. In the absence of a transatlantic policy approach toward the Asia Pacific, these divergences will persist and deepen, particularly as the region significantly shapes the global economy and confronts the challenges to its security architecture.

This report sought to highlight the costs of missed transatlantic policy opportunities in the region while seeking to develop a new transatlantic roadmap to encourage policy convergence on future opportunities. The policy recommendations we offer in the body of this report highlight specific areas where enhanced transatlantic consultation can help not only to reduce policy divergence but to more effectively focus policy engagement and deploy budgetary resources to strengthen regional cooperation. Clearly, the most important first step is for the transatlantic community to prioritize the Asia-Pacific region as a critical area of cooperation in its ongoing dialogue. Structured EU-U.S. dialogues must be created, particularly in the economic and trade and investment space. There must be a clear sense of urgency to develop U.S.-EU consultations related to granting China Market Economy Status, as well as to the formation of a joint statement on the Outcome of the Tribunal of the Permanent Arbitration Court in the Hague. Should the United States and European Union seize these two important opportunities, one could begin to see the outlines of a transatlantic policy toward the Asia-Pacific region emerge. Should the transatlantic partners maintain differing policies, however, the West would fail once again to uphold, support, and export the international rules-based order and values system that it created to this vital region.

# About the Authors

**Heather A. Conley** is senior vice president for Europe, Eurasia, and the Arctic and director of the Europe Program at CSIS. Prior to joining CSIS in 2009, she served as executive director of the Office of the Chairman of the Board at the American National Red Cross. From 2001 to 2005, she served as deputy assistant secretary of state in the Bureau for European and Eurasian Affairs with responsibilities for U.S. bilateral relations with the countries of northern and central Europe. From 1994 to 2001, she was a senior associate with an international consulting firm led by former U.S. deputy secretary of state Richard L. Armitage. Ms. Conley began her career in the Bureau of Political-Military Affairs at the U.S. Department of State. She was selected to serve as special assistant to the coordinator of U.S. assistance to the newly independent states of the former Soviet Union. Ms. Conley is a member of the World Economic Forum's Global Agenda Council on the Arctic and is frequently featured as a foreign policy analyst on CNN, MSNBC, BBC, NPR, and PBS. She received her B.A. in international studies from West Virginia Wesleyan College and her M.A. in international relations from the Johns Hopkins University School of Advanced International Studies (SAIS).

**James Mina** is a research associate with the CSIS Europe Program, where he oversees the program's portfolio covering European integration, the European political economy, and transatlantic security issues. Mina first joined the CSIS Europe Program as a research intern in fall 2012 and returned as a member of the program staff in 2013. Since then, his primary research focus has been dedicated to analyzing Southern and Southeastern European affairs and the political and economic aftershocks of the sovereign debt crisis, as well as understanding the impact of Russian influence in Central and Eastern Europe. He recently coauthored a CSIS report, *Understanding the European Consequences of a Modern Greek Odyssey*, and has also been published in *Survival*. He received an M.A. in international relations and economics from the Johns Hopkins University School of Advanced International Studies (SAIS), with a concentration in conflict management, and obtained a B.A. magna cum laude from the College of the Holy Cross. He is proficient in Italian.

**Phuong Nguyen** is an associate fellow with the Chair for Southeast Asia Studies at CSIS. In this role, she leads the Chair's research team, writes on Southeast Asia, U.S. foreign policy toward countries in the Association of Southeast Asian Nations (ASEAN), and China's peripheral diplomacy. Nguyen is a coauthor of *Building a More Robust U.S.-Philippines Alliance* (CSIS, August 2015), *Southeast Asia's Geopolitical Centrality and the U.S.-Japan Alliance* (CSIS, June 2015), *Thailand in Crisis: Scenarios and Policy Responses* (CSIS, July 2014), and *A New Era in U.S.-Vietnam Relations: Deepening Ties Two Decades after Normalization* (CSIS, June 2014). She is a coeditor of *Examining the South China Sea Disputes* (CSIS, November 2015) and *Perspectives on the South China Sea: Diplomatic, Legal, and Security Dimensions of the Dispute* (CSIS, September 2014). Her work has been published in *East Asia Forum*, *Yale Global*, *World Politics Review*, *Nikkei Asian Review*, *The Straits Times*, *Bangkok Post*, and *Business Insider*. Nguyen holds an M.A. in Asian studies from the School of International Service at American University in Washington, D.C. She speaks fluent French and Vietnamese.

www.ingramcontent.com/pod-product-compliance
Lightning Source LLC
Chambersburg PA
CBHW081438270326
41932CB00019B/3252